SAGAR KALE

SwiftUI Basics in 1 Day

Jump into SwiftUI future of Swift

Contents

1

Learning SwiftUI

Learning SwiftUI concepts step by step is a great approach to understanding the framework and building proficiency in creating user interfaces for Apple platforms. Here's a suggested step-by-step guide:

1. Get Familiar with Swift:

- Ensure you have a good understanding of the Swift programming language, as SwiftUI is built on top of Swift.
- Learn about Swift syntax, data types, control flow, and functions.

2. Learn the Basics of SwiftUI:

- Understand the basic structure of a SwiftUI application.
- Create simple SwiftUI views using built-in components like **Text**, **Image**, and **Button**.

3. Modifiers:

- Explore modifiers to customize the appearance and behavior of SwiftUI views.
- Learn how to chain modifiers to create complex UIs with minimal code.

4. Layout and Stacks:

- Understand layout in SwiftUI using stacks (**VStack**, **HStack**, **ZStack**).
- Explore alignment, spacing, and distribution within stacks.

5. State and Data Flow:

- Introduce the concept of **@State** for managing local state within a view.
- Learn how to update views dynamically based on changes in state.

6. User Interaction:

- Handle user interactions using gestures and controls (e.g., **Button**, **TextField**, **Toggle**).
- Explore how to bind user input to state variables.

7. Navigation:

- Learn how to navigate between views using **NavigationView** and **NavigationLink**.
- Understand how to pass data between views.

8. Lists and Navigation:

- Explore the **List** view for displaying dynamic content.
- Learn to navigate within lists and present details.

9. Combine Framework Integration:

- Understand the basics of the Combine framework for handling asynchronous operations and data streams.
- Integrate Combine with SwiftUI for reactive programming.

10. Advanced UI Components:

- Explore more advanced UI components like **Form**, **Picker**, and **DatePicker**.
- Learn how to create custom views and modifiers.

11. Animation:

- Understand animation principles in SwiftUI.
- Animate view transitions and state changes.

12. Accessibility:

- Learn about making your SwiftUI apps accessible.
- Implement features for users with different accessibility needs.

13. Testing and Debugging:

- Explore testing techniques for SwiftUI views and view models.
- Learn to use SwiftUI previews for rapid prototyping.

14. Combine Advanced Topics:

- Explore advanced Combine concepts like custom publishers and operators.
- Understand error handling and cancellation.

15. Integration with UIKit and App Architecture:

- Learn how to integrate SwiftUI with existing UIKit code.
- Understand how SwiftUI fits into different app architectures.

16. Real-world Projects:

- Apply your knowledge by building small to medium-sized projects.
- Experiment with SwiftUI in personal or open-source projects.

17. Community and Resources:

- Engage with the SwiftUI community through forums, blogs, and social media.
- Stay updated with SwiftUI-related announcements from Apple.

Remember to practice regularly, build projects, and refer to the official Apple documentation and community resources for the latest updates and best practices. SwiftUI is a powerful framework, and hands-on experience is crucial for mastering it.

Create simple SwiftUI views using built-in components like Text, Image, and Button

Certainly! Below is a simple SwiftUI example that demonstrates the use of basic components like **Text**, **Image**, and **Button**. This example creates a basic view with a text label, an image, and a button:

```
import SwiftUI

struct ContentView: View {
    var body: some View {
        VStack {
            // Text View
```

```
Text("Hello, SwiftUI!")
    .font(.title)
    .foregroundColor(.blue)

// Image View
Image(systemName: "swift")
    .resizable()
    .scaledToFit()
    .frame(width: 100, height: 100)
    .padding()

// Button
Button(action: {
    // Action to perform when the button
    is tapped
    print("Button tapped!")
}) {
    Text("Tap me!")
        .foregroundColor(.white)
        .padding()
        .background(Color.green)
        .cornerRadius(10)
    }
  }
    .padding()
  }
}

// Preview the ContentView
import PlaygroundSupport
PlaygroundPage.current.setLiveView(ContentView())
```

In this example:

- The **Text** view displays a simple text message with a larger font and blue color.

- The **Image** view uses the system symbol "swift" and is resizable, with a fixed width and height.
- The **Button** view contains a text label ("Tap me!") and is styled with custom foreground and background colors.

You can run this code in a SwiftUI-supported environment like Xcode's SwiftUI Playground or integrate it into a SwiftUI project. Feel free to modify and experiment with the code to get a hands-on understanding of SwiftUI's declarative syntax and how it allows you to create and customize user interfaces with ease.

2

Modifiers:

Modifiers:

In SwiftUI, modifiers are used to customize the appearance and behavior of views. You apply modifiers to views to change their properties, such as color, font, padding, and more. Modifiers are chained together to create a sequence of transformations, allowing you to express the desired look and behavior of your UI in a concise and readable manner.

Here's an overview of some common modifiers and how they can be used:

```
import SwiftUI

struct ContentView: View {
    var body: some View {
        VStack {
            // Text View with Modifiers
```

```
Text("Hello, SwiftUI!")
    .font(.title)
    // Set the font size
    .foregroundColor(.blue)
    // Set the text color
    .padding()
    // Add padding around the text
    .background(Color.yellow)          //
    Set a background color
    .cornerRadius(10)
    // Round the corners

// Image View with Modifiers
Image(systemName: "star.fill")
    .resizable()
    // Allow the image to be resized
    .scaledToFit()
    // Scale the image to fit its frame
    .frame(width: 50, height: 50)      //
    Set a fixed width and height
    .padding()
    // Add padding around the image
    .foregroundColor(.orange)
    // Set the image color

// Button with Modifiers
Button(action: {
    // Action to perform when the button
    is tapped
    print("Button tapped!")
}) {
    Text("Tap me!")
        .padding()
        // Add padding around the button
        text
        .background(Color.green)
        // Set the button background color
```

9

```
                    .foregroundColor(.white)
                    // Set the button text color
                    .cornerRadius(10)
                    // Round the corners
            }
        }
        .padding()
        // Add padding around the VStack
    }
}

// Preview the ContentView
import PlaygroundSupport
PlaygroundPage.current.setLiveView(ContentView())
```

In this example:

- For the **Text** view, modifiers like **font, foregroundColor, padding, background,** and **cornerRadius** are applied to customize its appearance.
- The **Image** view uses modifiers like **resizable, scaledToFit, frame, padding,** and **foregroundColor** to customize its appearance.
- The **Button** view is customized with modifiers for **padding, background, foregroundColor,** and **cornerRadius.**

Experimenting with modifiers is a great way to understand how SwiftUI enables you to create expressive and dynamic user interfaces with minimal code.

Learn how to create custom views and modifiers.

Certainly! In SwiftUI, creating custom views and modifiers allows you to encapsulate reusable components and styling for your UI. Here's a brief guide on how to create custom views and modifiers:

Creating Custom Views:

1. **Create a New SwiftUI View:** Start by creating a new SwiftUI view. You can do this by creating a new Swift file and adopting the **View** protocol.

```
import SwiftUI

struct CustomView: View {
    var body: some View {
        // Your view content here
        Text("Hello, Custom View!")
    }
}
```

1. **Use the Custom View in ContentView:** You can now use your custom view in other SwiftUI views, such as **ContentView**.

```
struct ContentView: View {
    var body: some View {
        VStack {
            CustomView()
            Text("Other content in ContentView")
        }
    }
}
```

Creating Custom Modifiers:

1. **Create a New SwiftUI Modifier:** Modifiers in SwiftUI are functions that return a modified version of a view. Create a new Swift file and define your custom modifier.

```
import SwiftUI

struct CustomModifier: ViewModifier {
    func body(content: Content) -> some View {
        content
            .foregroundColor(.blue)
            .padding()
            .background(Color.yellow)
            .cornerRadius(10)
    }
}
```

1. **Apply the Custom Modifier:** You can then use your custom modifier with any SwiftUI view to apply the defined styling.

```
struct ContentView: View {
    var body: some View {
        Text("Hello, Custom Modifier!")
            .modifier(CustomModifier())
    }
}
```

Combining Custom Views and Modifiers:

You can combine custom views and modifiers to create more complex and reusable components.

```
struct CustomComponent: View {
    var body: some View {
        VStack {
            CustomView()
                .modifier(CustomModifier())
            Text("Other content in CustomComponent")
        }
    }
}
```

This is a basic example, and you can make your custom views and modifiers more sophisticated based on your application's needs. SwiftUI's declarative syntax allows you to compose complex UIs by combining and nesting these custom components and modifiers.

3

Layout and Stacks:

Layout and Stacks:

In SwiftUI, layout is structured using stacks, which are container views that arrange their child views either horizontally (HStack), vertically (VStack), or overlaid on top of each other (ZStack). Stacks are fundamental for building the structure of your user interface. Let's take a look at how to use layout and stacks in SwiftUI:

```
import SwiftUI

struct ContentView: View {
    var body: some View {
        VStack {
            // Vertical Stack (VStack)
            Text("Top View")
                .padding()
                .background(Color.blue)
```

LAYOUT AND STACKS:

```swift
HStack {
    // Horizontal Stack (HStack)
    Text("Left View")
        .padding()
        .background(Color.green)

    Spacer() // Spacer to push the next
    view to the right

    Text("Right View")
        .padding()
        .background(Color.yellow)
}

ZStack {
    // ZStack (Overlay)
    Text("Center View")
        .padding()
        .background(Color.red)
}

Spacer() // Spacer to push the next view
to the bottom

// Another Vertical Stack (VStack)
Text("Bottom View")
    .padding()
    .background(Color.purple)
        }
        .padding()
    }
}

// Preview the ContentView
import PlaygroundSupport
PlaygroundPage.current.setLiveView(ContentView())
```

In this example:

- A **VStack** is used as the main container. Inside it, you find several child views arranged vertically.
- The first child is a **Text** view within a **VStack** to create a vertical stack.
- The second child is an **HStack** containing two **Text** views, creating a horizontal stack.
- The third child is a **ZStack** containing a single **Text** view, creating an overlay stack.
- A **Spacer** is used to push the right view to the right within the **HStack**.
- Another **Spacer** is used to push the bottom view to the bottom within the main **VStack**.

Experimenting with different combinations of **VStack**, **HStack**, and **ZStack**, along with spacers, allows you to create flexible and dynamic layouts in SwiftUI. Stacks make it easy to organize and structure your UI, and they play a key role in building responsive interfaces for various Apple platforms.

4

State and Data Flow:

State and Data Flow:

In SwiftUI, state management is a critical concept for building dynamic and interactive user interfaces. The **@State** property wrapper is used to declare and manage the state of a view. When the state changes, SwiftUI automatically re-renders the affected parts of the view to reflect those changes. Let's explore how to use **@State** for managing state and facilitating data flow in SwiftUI:

```
import SwiftUI

struct ContentView: View {
    // Declare a state variable
    @State private var counter = 0

    var body: some View {
```

```
VStack {
    // Display the counter value
    Text("Counter: \(counter)")
        .font(.title)

    // Button to increment the counter
    Button("Increment") {
        // Update the state variable
        counter += 1
    }
    .padding()
    }
  }
}

// Preview the ContentView
import PlaygroundSupport
PlaygroundPage.current.setLiveView(ContentView())
```

In this example:

- **@State private var counter = 0** declares a state variable named **counter** with an initial value of 0. The **@State** property wrapper tells SwiftUI to manage the state for this variable.
- The **Text** view displays the value of the **counter** state.
- The **Button** view has an action associated with it. When the button is tapped, the action is executed, updating the **counter** state.
- SwiftUI automatically re-renders the view when the state changes, ensuring that the displayed counter is always up to date.

This mechanism of using **@State** for local view state is a fundamental pattern in SwiftUI. For more complex scenarios or when sharing state between different views, you may explore other property wrappers like **@Binding, @ObservedObject**, and **@EnvironmentObject**.

Binding:

You can also pass a binding to a child view to establish a two-way connection between the parent and child views. Here's a simple example:

```
import SwiftUI

struct ContentView: View {
    @State private var counter = 0

    var body: some View {
        VStack {
            Text("Counter: \(counter)")
                .font(.title)

            ChildView(counter: $counter) // Pass a
            binding to the child view
        }
    }
}

struct ChildView: View {
    @Binding var counter: Int // Declare a binding to
    the counter state

    var body: some View {
        Button("Increment in Child") {
            counter += 1 // Update the counter
```

```
        through the binding
    }
    .padding()
  }
}
```

In this example, the **ChildView** receives a binding to the **counter** state. When the button is tapped in the child view, it updates the counter through the binding, and the parent view gets automatically updated as well.

Understanding state and data flow is crucial for building responsive and interactive SwiftUI applications. Experimenting with these concepts in small projects or playgrounds will help solidify your understanding.

Understand how to pass data between views.

In SwiftUI, you can pass data between views using various methods, depending on your application's structure and requirements. Here are some common approaches to pass data between views:

1. Using @State:

You can use **@State** to manage the state of a view and indirectly pass data to child views. This is suitable for simple data sharing within the view hierarchy.

Example:

```
import SwiftUI

struct ContentView: View {
    @State private var username = ""

    var body: some View {
        VStack {
            TextField("Enter username", text:
            $username)
            ChildView(username: $username)
        }
    }
}

struct ChildView: View {
    @Binding var username: String

    var body: some View {
        Text("Hello, \(username)!")
    }
}
```

2. Using @Binding:

When you need two-way communication between parent and child views, you can use **@Binding**.

Example:

```
import SwiftUI
```

```
struct ContentView: View {
    @State private var username = ""

    var body: some View {
        VStack {
            TextField("Enter username", text:
            $username)
            ChildView(username: $username)
        }
    }
}

struct ChildView: View {
    @Binding var username: String

    var body: some View {
        Text("Hello, \(username)!")
    }
}
```

3. Using EnvironmentObject:

For sharing data across multiple views, you can use an **Observ-ableObject** with **@EnvironmentObject**. This is suitable for more complex scenarios.

Example:

```
import SwiftUI

class UserData: ObservableObject {
    @Published var username = ""
}
```

```
struct ContentView: View {
    @EnvironmentObject var userData: UserData

    var body: some View {
        VStack {
            TextField("Enter username", text:
            $userData.username)
            ChildView()
        }
    }
}

struct ChildView: View {
    @EnvironmentObject var userData: UserData

    var body: some View {
        Text("Hello, \(userData.username)!")
    }
}
```

4. Using @StateObject and @ObservedObject:

In SwiftUI, you can use **@StateObject** for creating a view-specific instance of an **ObservableObject**, and **@ObservedObject** to observe changes in the object.

  Example:

```
import SwiftUI

class UserData: ObservableObject {
    @Published var username = ""
}
```

```
struct ContentView: View {
    @StateObject private var userData = UserData()

    var body: some View {
        VStack {
            TextField("Enter username", text:
            $userData.username)
            ChildView(userData: userData)
        }
    }
}

struct ChildView: View {
    @ObservedObject var userData: UserData

    var body: some View {
        Text("Hello, \(userData.username)!")
    }
}
```

Choose the approach that best fits your application's architecture and requirements. These methods allow you to pass and share data between views in a SwiftUI application.

5

User Interaction:

Handle user interactions using gestures and controls (e.g., Button, TextField, Toggle).

In SwiftUI, handling user interactions involves using gestures and controls to create responsive and interactive user interfaces. Here's a simple example that demonstrates how to use a **Button**, **TextField**, and **Toggle** to handle user interactions:

```
import SwiftUI

struct ContentView: View {
    @State private var tappedMessage: String =
    "Button not tapped"
    @State private var enteredText: String = ""
    @State private var isToggleOn: Bool = false

    var body: some View {
        VStack {
```

```
// Button with Tap Gesture
Button(action: {
    // Action to perform when the button
    is tapped
    tappedMessage = "Button tapped!"
}) {
    Text("Tap Me!")
        .padding()
        .foregroundColor(.white)
        .background(Color.blue)
        .cornerRadius(10)
}
.padding()

// Display the tapped message
Text(tappedMessage)
    .padding()

// TextField for Text Input
TextField("Enter text", text:
$enteredText)
    .textFieldStyle(RoundedBorderTextFieldStyle())
    .padding()

// Display the entered text
Text("Entered Text: \(enteredText)")
    .padding()

// Toggle for On/Off state
Toggle("Toggle", isOn: $isToggleOn)
    .padding()

// Display the toggle state
Text("Toggle is \(isToggleOn ? "On" :
"Off")")
    .padding()
}
```

```
    }
}

// Preview the ContentView
import PlaygroundSupport
PlaygroundPage.current.setLiveView(ContentView())
```

In this example:

1. **Button:**

- The **Button** view is created with a closure that updates the **tappedMessage** state when tapped.
- The **tappedMessage** state is displayed below the button to show the result.

1. **TextField:**

- The **TextField** view is used to capture user input. It is bound to the **enteredText** state.
- The entered text is displayed below the text field.

1. **Toggle:**

- The **Toggle** view is used to represent an on/off state. It is bound to the **isToggleOn** state.
- The state of the toggle is displayed below the toggle switch.

Feel free to interact with the UI elements in a SwiftUI-supported environment like Xcode's SwiftUI Playground or integrate the code into a SwiftUI project. Experimenting with different gestures and controls will help you understand how to handle user interactions and update the state of your views accordingly.

Explore how to bind user input to state variables.

In SwiftUI, you can bind user input to state variables using various controls like **TextField**, **Toggle**, **Picker**, etc. This allows the user interface to reflect and interact with the underlying data. Here's an example demonstrating how to bind user input to state variables using a **TextField** and a **Toggle**:

```swift
import SwiftUI

struct ContentView: View {
    @State private var enteredText: String = ""
    @State private var isToggleOn: Bool = false

    var body: some View {
        VStack {
            // TextField for Text Input
            TextField("Enter text", text:
            $enteredText)
                .textFieldStyle(RoundedBorderTextFieldStyle())
                .padding()

            // Display the entered text
            Text("Entered Text: \(enteredText)")
                .padding()
```

```
        // Toggle for On/Off state
        Toggle("Toggle", isOn: $isToggleOn)
            .padding()

        // Display the toggle state
        Text("Toggle is \(isToggleOn ? "On" :
        "Off")")
            .padding()
    }
    .padding()
}
}

// Preview the ContentView
import PlaygroundSupport
PlaygroundPage.current.setLiveView(ContentView())
```

In this example:

1. **TextField:**

- The **TextField** view is used to capture user input, and it is bound to the **enteredText** state variable using the **$** prefix.
- As the user types in the text field, the **enteredText** state is automatically updated, and the displayed text reflects the entered value.

1. **Toggle:**

- The **Toggle** view represents an on/off state, and it is bound to the **isToggleOn** state variable.
- As the user interacts with the toggle switch, the **isToggleOn**

state is updated accordingly, and the displayed text reflects the state.

Binding user input to state variables simplifies the management of data flow within your SwiftUI views. This declarative approach ensures that the UI is always synchronized with the underlying data, and changes to the data are immediately reflected in the user interface.

6

Navigation:

Learn how to navigate between views using NavigationView and NavigationLink.

In SwIftUI, navigation between views is achieved using **NavigationView** and **NavigationLink**. **NavigationView** provides a navigation container, and **NavigationLink** allows you to define a link from one view to another. Here's a simple example demonstrating how to navigate between views using these components:

```
import SwiftUI

struct ContentView: View {
    var body: some View {
        NavigationView {
            VStack {
```

```
                // View 1
                NavigationLink(destination:
                SecondView()) {
                    Text("Go to Second View")
                        .padding()
                        .background(Color.blue)
                        .foregroundColor(.white)
                        .cornerRadius(10)
                }
                .padding()

                // Other content in the first view
                Text("This is the First View")
                        .padding()
            }
            .navigationTitle("First View")
        }
    }
}

struct SecondView: View {
    var body: some View {
        VStack {
            // View 2
            Text("This is the Second View")
                .padding()

            // Other content in the second view
            NavigationLink(destination: ThirdView()) {
                Text("Go to Third View")
                    .padding()
                    .background(Color.green)
                    .foregroundColor(.white)
                    .cornerRadius(10)
            }
            .padding()
        }
```

```
            .navigationTitle("Second View")
        }
    }

struct ThirdView: View {
    var body: some View {
        // View 3
        Text("This is the Third View")
            .padding()
            .navigationTitle("Third View")
    }
}

// Preview the ContentView
import PlaygroundSupport
PlaygroundPage.current.setLiveView(ContentView())
```

In this example:

1. The main view (**ContentView**) is embedded in a **NavigationView**.
2. **NavigationLink** is used to create a link from the first view to the second view. When the user taps the "Go to Second View" button, it navigates to the **SecondView**.
3. **SecondView** contains a similar **NavigationLink** to navigate to the **ThirdView**.
4. Each view sets its own title using the **.navigationTitle** modifier.
5. The **PlaygroundPage** is used to preview the **ContentView**.

When working in a SwiftUI project in Xcode, you would typically use the **NavigationView** and **NavigationLink** within the context of a SwiftUI **List**, **ForEach**, or other navigation scenarios.

This basic example demonstrates the fundamental structure of navigation in SwiftUI. You can further customize navigation transitions, handle back navigation, and pass data between views as your application grows.

7

Lists and Navigation

Lists and Navigation: Explore the List view for displaying dynamic content.

In SwiftUI, the **List** view is a powerful container for displaying dynamic content, especially when dealing with collections of data. It automatically manages the display and layout of a dynamic collection, making it easy to create scrollable lists. Here's an example demonstrating the use of **List** and navigation in SwiftUI:

```
import SwiftUI

struct ContentView: View {
    var body: some View {
        NavigationView {
            List {
                ForEach(1..<6) { index in
```

```
            // Each row in the list
            NavigationLink(destination:
            DetailView(itemNumber: index)) {
                Text("Item \(index)")
            }
        }
    }
    .navigationTitle("List and Navigation")
        }
    }
}

struct DetailView: View {
    let itemNumber: Int

    var body: some View {
        VStack {
            Text("Detail View for Item \(itemNumber)")
            // Additional details or content for each
            item
        }
        .navigationTitle("Item \(itemNumber)")
    }
}

// Preview the ContentView
import PlaygroundSupport
PlaygroundPage.current.setLiveView(ContentView())
```

In this example:

- The **List** is used to display a dynamic collection of items. The **ForEach** loop generates rows in the list for each item.
- Each row is a **Text** view representing an item, and a **Navigation-Link** is used to navigate to a detailed view (**DetailView**)

36

when tapped.
- The **DetailView** is a simple view that displays additional details for the selected item.
- The **NavigationView** provides the navigation structure, and the **.navigationTitle** modifier sets the title for each view.

You can customize the **List** with various styles, including grouped lists, inset lists, and more. Additionally, you can include other SwiftUI views, such as images, buttons, or additional text, within the rows of the list to create more complex and informative layouts.

This example provides a basic introduction to using **List** and navigation in SwiftUI. As your application grows, you may encounter scenarios where you want to customize the appearance and behavior of list items, handle selection events, or add more advanced features.

Learn to navigate within lists and present details.

In SwiftUI, you can navigate within lists and present details by using the **NavigationLink** within a **List**. Here's an example that demonstrates navigating within a list and presenting details when an item is selected:

```
import SwiftUI
```

```
struct ContentView: View {
    var body: some View {
        NavigationView {
            List {
                ForEach(1..<6) { index in
                    // Each row in the list with a
                    NavigationLink
                    NavigationLink(destination:
                    DetailView(itemNumber: index)) {
                        Text("Item \(index)")
                    }
                }
            }
            .navigationTitle("List Navigation
            Example")
        }
    }
}

struct DetailView: View {
    let itemNumber: Int

    var body: some View {
        VStack {
            Text("Details for Item \(itemNumber)")
            // Additional details or content for each
            item
        }
        .navigationTitle("Item \(itemNumber)")
    }
}

// Preview the ContentView
import PlaygroundSupport
PlaygroundPage.current.setLiveView(ContentView())
```

In this example:

- The **List** contains a series of **NavigationLink** elements, each representing an item in the list.
- The **NavigationView** is used to set up the navigation structure.
- When a user taps on a row in the list, it triggers the **NavigationLink** to navigate to the **DetailView** for that specific item.
- The **DetailView** displays additional details or content for the selected item.
- The **.navigationTitle** modifier is used to set titles for each view.

You can customize the appearance of the list, handle selection events, and add more advanced features based on your application's requirements. This is a fundamental pattern in SwiftUI for navigating within lists and presenting details, and it's commonly used in iOS applications for presenting hierarchical content.

Experiment with the code in a SwiftUI-supported environment like Xcode or a SwiftUI Playground to see the navigation in action and to customize it further based on your specific needs.

8

Combine Framework Integration

Combine Framework Integration: Understand the basics of the Combine framework for handling asynchronous operations and data streams.

Combine is a framework introduced by Apple that provides a declarative Swift API for processing values over time. It's particularly powerful for handling asynchronous operations and managing data streams. Combine introduces a set of publishers and operators that allow you to work with asynchronous and event-driven code in a more functional and reactive way.

Here are some key concepts and components of the Combine framework:

Publishers and Subscribers:

- **Publisher:** A publisher is an object that emits a sequence of values over time. It can represent a stream of events, such as network requests, user inputs, or changes in state.
- **Subscriber:** A subscriber is an object that receives and processes the values emitted by a publisher. It subscribes to a publisher and defines how to handle the received values.

Operators:

Combine provides a set of operators that allow you to transform, filter, and combine values emitted by publishers. Some common operators include **map**, **filter**, **merge**, **combineLatest**, and more.

Cancellable:

A subscription to a publisher returns a **Cancellable** object. You can use this object to cancel the subscription and stop receiving updates from the publisher.

Example:

Here's a simple example demonstrating the use of Combine to handle asynchronous operations:

```
import Combine

// Define a simple publisher that emits values over
time
let publisher = Timer.publish(every: 1, on: .main,
```

```
in: .default)
    .autoconnect()
    .map { _ in "Tick" }

// Define a subscriber to receive and print the values
let cancellable = publisher.sink { value in
    print(value)
}

// Cancel the subscription after 5 seconds
DispatchQueue.main.asyncAfter(deadline: .now() + 5) {
    cancellable.cancel()
}
```

In this example:

- **Timer.publish** creates a publisher that emits values at regular intervals.
- **map** transforms the emitted values to "Tick".
- **sink** subscribes to the publisher and prints each received value.
- The subscription is canceled after 5 seconds.

Combine is extensively used in SwiftUI for handling asynchronous tasks, updating UI based on data changes, and more. It's a powerful tool for dealing with asynchronous and reactive programming in Swift. You can explore more advanced concepts like error handling, subjects, and custom publishers as you become more familiar with Combine.

Integrate Combine with SwiftUI for reactive programming.

Integrating Combine with SwiftUI is a powerful way to achieve reactive programming and handle asynchronous tasks in your SwiftUI applications. Combine provides a set of publishers and operators that seamlessly integrate with SwiftUI's data flow, making it easier to manage state, handle asynchronous operations, and update UI components. Below is a simple example that demonstrates how to use Combine with SwiftUI:

```swift
import SwiftUI
import Combine

// Define a simple view model with a Combine publisher
class ViewModel: ObservableObject {
    @Published var counter = 0

    // A Combine publisher that emits values when the
    counter changes
    var counterPublisher: AnyPublisher<Int, Never> {
        $counter.eraseToAnyPublisher()
    }

    // Function to increment the counter
    func increment() {
        counter += 1
    }
}

struct ContentView: View {
    // Inject the view model
    @ObservedObject var viewModel: ViewModel
```

```swift
    // State variable to hold the latest counter
    value from the publisher
    @State private var latestCounter = 0

    // Combine cancellable to manage the subscription
    private var cancellable: AnyCancellable?

    init(viewModel: ViewModel) {
        self.viewModel = viewModel

        // Subscribe to the counter publisher and
        update the state variable
        cancellable = viewModel.counterPublisher
            .assign(to: \.latestCounter, on: self)
    }

    var body: some View {
        VStack {
            Text("Counter: \(latestCounter)")
                .font(.title)
                .padding()

            Button("Increment") {
                // Call the increment function in the
                view model
                viewModel.increment()
            }
            .padding()
        }
    }
}

// Create an instance of the ViewModel
let viewModel = ViewModel()

// Create and preview the ContentView with the
ViewModel
```

```
let contentView = ContentView(viewModel: viewModel)
PlaygroundPage.current.setLiveView(contentView)
```

In this example:

- **ViewModel** is an **ObservableObject** class with a **@Published** property **counter**. The **counterPublisher** property exposes a Combine publisher for the counter.
- **ContentView** is a SwiftUI view that observes changes to the **latestCounter** state variable. It subscribes to the **counter-Publisher** in the view model and updates the UI whenever the counter changes.
- The **Button** in the view triggers the **increment** function in the view model, which updates the **counter** property.
- The Combine **assign(to:on:)** operator is used to assign values from the publisher to the **latestCounter** state variable.

This is a basic example, and Combine can be used for more complex scenarios, such as handling network requests, debouncing user input, chaining asynchronous operations, and more. Combining Combine with SwiftUI simplifies the handling of data flow and state management in your applications.

9

Advanced UI Components

Advanced UI Components: Explore more advanced UI components like Form, Picker, and DatePicker.

Certainly! In SwiftUI, there are advanced UI components that help in creating sophisticated and interactive user interfaces. Let's explore the usage of **Form**, **Picker**, and **DatePicker**:

Form:

Form is a container view that is used to group related controls together. It is commonly used for creating settings pages or any other form-based user interfaces.

```
import SwiftUI

struct ContentView: View {
    var body: some View {
```

```
NavigationView {
    Form {
        Section(header: Text("Personal
        Information")) {
            TextField("First Name", text:
            .constant(""))
            TextField("Last Name", text:
            .constant(""))
        }

        Section(header: Text("Account
        Settings")) {
            Toggle("Receive Notifications",
            isOn: .constant(true))
            Stepper("Preferred Number of
            Items", value: .constant(5), in:
            1...10)
        }

        Section {
            Button("Save Changes") {
                // Handle save action
            }
        }
    }
    .navigationTitle("Settings")
    }
}
}

// Preview the ContentView
import PlaygroundSupport
PlaygroundPage.current.setLiveView(ContentView())
```

In this example, a **Form** is used to organize a series of controls into sections. Each section has a header, and controls like

TextField, **Toggle**, and **Stepper** are used to collect user input.

Picker:

Picker is a view that allows the user to make selections from a set of options.

```swift
import SwiftUI

struct ContentView: View {
    @State private var selectedColor = "Red"
    let colors = ["Red", "Green", "Blue", "Yellow"]

    var body: some View {
        VStack {
            Picker("Select a Color", selection:
            $selectedColor) {
                ForEach(colors, id: \.self) {
                    Text($0)
                }
            }
            .pickerStyle(WheelPickerStyle())

            Text("Selected Color: \(selectedColor)")
                .padding()
        }
        .padding()
    }
}

// Preview the ContentView
import PlaygroundSupport
PlaygroundPage.current.setLiveView(ContentView())
```

In this example, a **Picker** is used to allow the user to select a color from the options defined in the **colors** array. The selected value is bound to the **selectedColor** state variable.

DatePicker:

DatePicker is a view that allows the user to pick a date and/or time.

```
import SwiftUI

struct ContentView: View {
    @State private var selectedDate = Date()

    var body: some View {
        VStack {
            DatePicker("Select a Date", selection:
            $selectedDate, displayedComponents:
            [.date, .hourAndMinute])
                .datePickerStyle(GraphicalDatePickerStyle())

            Text("Selected Date: \(selectedDate,
            formatter: DateFormatter.shortDateTime)")
                .padding()
        }
        .padding()
    }
}

extension DateFormatter {
    static var shortDateTime: DateFormatter {
        let formatter = DateFormatter()
        formatter.dateStyle = .short
        formatter.timeStyle = .short
        return formatter
    }
}
```

```
// Preview the ContentView
import PlaygroundSupport
PlaygroundPage.current.setLiveView(ContentView())
```

In this example, a **DatePicker** is used to allow the user to pick a date and time. The selected date is bound to the **selectedDate** state variable, and a custom date formatter is used to display the selected date and time.

These advanced UI components provide a wide range of options for creating rich and interactive user interfaces in SwiftUI. Experiment with these components and customize them based on your application's requirements.

10

Animation

Animation: Understand animation principles in SwiftUI.

In SwiftUI, animations are a powerful and integral part of creating engaging user interfaces. SwiftUI provides a declarative way to define and control animations seamlessly. Here are some key principles to understand about animations in SwiftUI:

1. **Declarative Syntax:** SwiftUI uses a declarative syntax to describe what the UI should look like in a certain state, and it automatically handles the animations between different states. Instead of specifying step-by-step instructions for animations, you declare the desired end state, and SwiftUI handles the transition.

2. **Animatable Values:** SwiftUI relies on animatable values to interpolate between different states. Most built-in SwiftUI components, like **Color**, **Opacity**, and **Offset**, are animatable. Additionally, you can create your custom ani-

matable properties by conforming to the **VectorArithmetic** protocol.

3. **Implicit vs. Explicit Animations:** SwiftUI supports both implicit and explicit animations. Implicit animations are applied automatically when a view's animatable properties change. For explicit animations, you can use the **withAnimation** modifier to animate changes within a specific block of code.

```
withAnimation {
    // Code with animated changes
}
```

1. **Animation Types:** SwiftUI supports various types of animations, including basic animations, spring animations, and more. The **animation** modifier allows you to specify the type of animation to use for a particular view or view hierarchy.

```
.animation(.easeInOut)
```

1. **Animation Stacks:** SwiftUI provides the **animation** modifier at different levels, allowing you to apply animations globally, for a specific view, or even for a specific transition.

```
.animation {
    Animation.easeInOut(duration: 0.5)
}
```

1. **Transitions:** SwiftUI makes it easy to apply transitions when views are added or removed. The **transition** modifier allows you to specify how a view enters or exits the view hierarchy.

```
.transition(.slide)
```

1. **Animating Bindings:** You can animate changes to **@State** or **@Binding** properties directly. When the value of a property changes, SwiftUI automatically animates the transition.

```
@State private var rotation: Double = 0.0

var body: some View {
    Image(systemName: "arrow.right.circle.fill")
        .rotationEffect(Angle(degrees: rotation))
        .onTapGesture {
            withAnimation {
                rotation += 45
            }
        }
}
```

1. **Animating Gesture Changes:** SwiftUI makes it easy to animate changes driven by gestures, such as dragging or tapping. Combine gestures with the **withAnimation** block for smooth transitions.

```
@State private var scale: CGFloat = 1.0

var body: some View {
    Image(systemName: "star.fill")
        .scaleEffect(scale)
        .gesture(
            MagnificationGesture()
                .onChanged { value in
                    withAnimation {
                        scale = value
                    }
                }
        )
}
```

Understanding these principles will help you create delightful animations in your SwiftUI applications. SwiftUI's approach to animations simplifies the process, making it easy to achieve smooth and visually appealing user interfaces.

Animate view transitions and state changes.

In SwiftUI, animating view transitions and state changes is an essential aspect of creating visually appealing and dynamic user interfaces. Here's how you can achieve animations for view transitions and state changes:

Animating View Transitions:

1. **Using the transition Modifier:** SwiftUI provides the **transition** modifier to animate view transitions when they appear or disappear. You can use predefined transition effects like **.opacity, .slide**, or create custom transitions.

```
struct ContentView: View {
    @State private var showText = false

    var body: some View {
        VStack {
            if showText {
                Text("Hello, SwiftUI!")
                    .transition(.slide)
            }
        }
        .onTapGesture {
            withAnimation {
                showText.toggle()
            }
        }
    }
}
```

1. **Customizing Transition Animations:** You can customize transition animations by combining the **animation** modi-

fier with the **transition** modifier. This allows you to control the duration, type, and other properties of the animation.

```
struct ContentView: View {
    @State private var showText = false

    var body: some View {
        VStack {
            if showText {
                Text("Hello, SwiftUI!")
                    .transition(.slide)
                    .animation(.easeInOut(duration:
                    1.0))
            }
        }
        .onTapGesture {
            withAnimation {
                showText.toggle()
            }
        }
    }
}
```

Animating State Changes:

1. **Using the withAnimation Block:** You can animate changes to **@State** variables using the **withAnimation** block. When the value of a **@State** variable changes inside the block, SwiftUI automatically animates the transition.

```
struct ContentView: View {
    @State private var scale: CGFloat = 1.0

    var body: some View {
        Image(systemName: "star.fill")
            .scaleEffect(scale)
            .onTapGesture {
                withAnimation {
                    scale = scale == 1.0 ? 1.5 : 1.0
                }
            }
    }
}
```

1. **Animating State Changes with Gestures:** You can integrate gestures with animations to create interactive animations. In the example below, a **DragGesture** is used to change the rotation angle with animation.

```
struct ContentView: View {
    @State private var rotation: Double = 0.0

    var body: some View {
        Image(systemName: "arrow.right.circle.fill")
            .rotationEffect(Angle(degrees: rotation))
            .gesture(
                DragGesture()
                    .onChanged { value in
                        withAnimation {
                            rotation =
                            value.translation.width /
                            5.0
                        }
```

```
                }
                .onEnded { _ in
                    withAnimation {
                        rotation = 0.0
                    }
                }
            )
        }
    }
```

These examples illustrate the basic principles of animating view transitions and state changes in SwiftUI. The key is to use the **withAnimation** block to wrap the changes you want to animate, and SwiftUI takes care of the rest, providing smooth and visually appealing animations.

11

Accessibility

Accessibility: Learn about making your SwiftUI apps accessible.

Accessibility is a crucial aspect of creating inclusive SwiftUI apps that can be used by people with diverse needs and abilities. SwiftUI provides built-in features to make your apps more accessible. Here are key considerations and practices for making SwiftUI apps accessible:

1. Labels and Hints:

- Use the **accessibility** modifiers to provide meaningful labels and hints for your views.
- For example, you can use **.accessibility(label: Text("Submit Button"))** to provide a label for a button.

2. Traits and Values:

- Specify accessibility traits and values to convey additional information about the purpose of a view.
- Use **.accessibility(addTraits: .isButton)** to indicate that a view behaves like a button.

3. Custom Accessibility Actions:

- Implement custom accessibility actions to enhance user interaction.
- Use **.accessibilityAction** to define custom actions triggered by accessibility gestures.

4. Dynamic Type:

- Design your app to support Dynamic Type, allowing users to adjust text size based on their preferences.
- Use the **.font** modifier with **.scaledFont** to automatically adjust font size based on the user's Dynamic Type setting.

5. Accessible Controls:

- Use standard SwiftUI controls like **Button, Toggle**, and **Slider**, as they come with built-in accessibility support.
- For custom controls, ensure they are accessible by providing appropriate labels and hints.

6. VoiceOver Testing:

- Test your app with VoiceOver to experience how it's used by users with visual impairments.
- Enable VoiceOver on your device or simulator and navigate through your app to ensure a positive experience.

7. Focus and Navigation:

- Implement accessibility navigation and ensure that users can navigate through your app using VoiceOver or other accessibility tools.
- Use **.focusable** and **.onMoveCommand** to control focus and navigation.

8. Accessibility Notifications:

- Use accessibility notifications to provide feedback about changes in your app.
- For example, use **.accessibilityNotification(.announcement)** to notify users about important updates.

9. Color Contrast:

- Ensure good color contrast for text and interactive elements to improve readability.
- Use the **.contrast** modifier to adapt your app's appearance based on accessibility settings.

10. Test on Real Devices:

```vbnet
vbnetCopy code
- Test your app on real devices with different
accessibility settings and configurations to identify
potential issues.
```

Example:

```swift
struct ContentView: View {
    var body: some View {
        Button("Submit") {
            // Action when the button is tapped
        }
        .foregroundColor(.white)
        .padding()
        .background(Color.blue)
        .cornerRadius(8)
        .accessibility(label: Text("Submit Button"))
        .accessibility(hint: Text("Tap to submit your
        form"))
        .accessibility(addTraits: .isButton)
    }
}
```

By following these accessibility practices, you can ensure that your SwiftUI app is usable and enjoyable for a broad audience, including individuals with different abilities and needs. Accessibility is not only about compliance; it also enhances the overall user experience for everyone.

12

Testing and Debugging

Testing and Debugging: Explore testing techniques for SwiftUI views and view models.

Testing SwiftUI views and view models is crucial for ensuring the reliability and correctness of your app. SwiftUI provides a testing framework that allows you to write unit tests for your views and view models. Here are some testing techniques for SwiftUI:

1. Unit Testing View Models:

- View models contain the business logic of your app. Write unit tests to validate the behavior of your view models.
- Test various scenarios, including edge cases and error conditions.
- Use XCTest assertions to verify that the expected outcomes match the actual outcomes.

Example of a View Model Test:

```
import XCTest
@testable import YourApp

class ViewModelTests: XCTestCase {

    func testIncrementCounter() {
        let viewModel = YourViewModel()
        viewModel.incrementCounter()

        XCTAssertEqual(viewModel.counter, 1)
    }

    // Add more test cases for different scenarios
}
```

2. PreviewProvider for Quick UI Previews:

- Use SwiftUI's **PreviewProvider** to create quick previews of your views during development.
- This allows you to visually inspect your views without running the app.

Example of PreviewProvider:

```
struct ContentView_Previews: PreviewProvider {
    static var previews: some View {
        ContentView()
    }
}
```

3. UI Testing:

- SwiftUI works seamlessly with Xcode's UI testing framework.
- Create UI tests to simulate user interactions and verify that your app behaves correctly.
- Test navigation, user inputs, and the correctness of UI elements.

Example of UI Testing:

```
import XCTest

class YourAppUITests: XCTestCase {

    func testExample() {
        let app = XCUIApplication()
        app.launch()

        // Perform UI actions and use XCTAssert to
        verify the outcomes
    }
}
```

4. Snapshot Testing:

- Use snapshot testing libraries like SnapshotTesting to capture and compare view snapshots.
- This helps ensure that UI changes do not introduce unintended visual changes.

Example of Snapshot Testing:

```
import XCTest
import SnapshotTesting
@testable import YourApp

class SnapshotTests: XCTestCase {

    func testContentView() {
        let contentView = ContentView()

        assertSnapshot(matching: contentView, as:
        .image)
    }
}
```

5. Combine Framework Testing:

- If your view models use Combine, test Combine publishers and subscribers to verify the flow of data.
- Use **XCTExpectFailure** to test error scenarios.

Example of Combine Testing:

```
import XCTest
import Combine
@testable import YourApp

class CombineTests: XCTestCase {
```

```
func testPublisher() {
    let viewModel = YourViewModel()
    let expectation =
    XCTestExpectation(description: "Completion
    triggered")

    var cancellables: Set<AnyCancellable> = []

    viewModel.$dataPublisher
        .sink(receiveCompletion: { _ in
            expectation.fulfill()
        }, receiveValue: { data in
            // Verify the received data
        })
        .store(in: &cancellables)

    // Perform actions that trigger the publisher

    wait(for: [expectation], timeout: 5.0)
    }
}
```

6. Mocking Dependencies:

- Use dependency injection to replace real dependencies with mock objects during testing.
- Mocking allows you to isolate the code you are testing and control its behavior.

Example of Mocking Dependencies:

```
protocol NetworkServiceProtocol {
    func fetchData(completion: @escaping
    (Result<Data, Error>) -> Void)
}

class MockNetworkService: NetworkServiceProtocol {
    func fetchData(completion: @escaping
    (Result<Data, Error>) -> Void) {
        // Return mock data or simulate network
        behavior
    }
}

class YourViewModel {
    var networkService: NetworkServiceProtocol

    init(networkService: NetworkServiceProtocol =
    MockNetworkService()) {
        self.networkService = networkService
    }
}
```

These testing techniques help ensure the reliability and correctness of your SwiftUI views and view models. Incorporate them into your development workflow to catch bugs early and build a robust app.

Learn to use SwiftUI previews for rapid prototyping.

SwiftUI previews are a powerful tool for rapid prototyping and development in Xcode. They allow you to quickly visualize and interact with your SwiftUI views without running the entire application. Here's how you can use SwiftUI previews for rapid prototyping:

1. Understanding PreviewProvider:

- SwiftUI views can conform to the **PreviewProvider** protocol, which allows you to create static previews of your views.
- Xcode automatically generates live previews that you can interact with in the canvas.

Example of a Basic PreviewProvider:

```
import SwiftUI

struct ContentView: View {
    var body: some View {
        Text("Hello, SwiftUI!")
    }
}

struct ContentView_Previews: PreviewProvider {
    static var previews: some View {
        ContentView()
    }
}
```

2. Previewing Different States:

- You can provide multiple previews with different states to visualize how your view looks in various scenarios.
- Use the **Group** to organize multiple previews.

Example of Multiple Previews:

```
struct ContentView_Previews: PreviewProvider {
    static var previews: some View {
        Group {
            ContentView()
            ContentView().foregroundColor(.red) //
            Different state
        }
    }
}
```

3. Previewing in Different Device Sizes:

- Use the **previewDevice** modifier to see how your views look on different devices.
- Xcode provides a list of device options in the preview canvas.

Example of Previewing in Different Devices:

```
struct ContentView_Previews: PreviewProvider {
    static var previews: some View {
        ContentView()
```

```
        .previewDevice(PreviewDevice(rawValue:
        "iPhone 12"))
    }
}
```

4. Previewing Dark Mode:

- Test how your views adapt to Dark Mode by using the **environment** modifier.
- Toggle between light and dark modes directly in the canvas.

Example of Previewing Dark Mode:

```
struct ContentView_Previews: PreviewProvider {
    static var previews: some View {
        ContentView()
            .environment(\.colorScheme, .dark)
    }
}
```

5. Previewing Dynamic Type:

- Check how your views respond to Dynamic Type changes by adjusting the **environment(\.sizeCategory)**.

Example of Previewing Dynamic Type:

```
struct ContentView_Previews: PreviewProvider {
    static var previews: some View {
        ContentView()
            .environment(\.sizeCategory, .extraLarge)
    }
}
```

6. Interactive Previews:

- SwiftUI previews are interactive, allowing you to interact with your views directly in the canvas.
- Test how your UI behaves with user interactions.

Example of Interactive Previews:

```
struct ContentView_Previews: PreviewProvider {
    static var previews: some View {
        ContentView()
            .previewInteraction { interaction in
                // Handle interactions for testing
            }
    }
}
```

7. Live Preview:

- Enable Live Preview by clicking the "Resume" button in the Xcode canvas.
- Changes made in the code are immediately reflected in the

live preview.

Example of Live Preview:

```
struct ContentView_Previews: PreviewProvider {
    static var previews: some View {
        ContentView()
            .foregroundColor(.green)
    }
}
```

By leveraging SwiftUI previews, you can rapidly iterate and prototype your UI, allowing for quick visualization and testing of different states and configurations. The live preview feature accelerates the development process by providing immediate feedback as you make changes to your code.

Understand error handling and cancellation.

Error handling and cancellation are important aspects of Combine, allowing you to handle issues that may arise during asynchronous operations and manage the lifecycle of subscriptions. Let's explore error handling and cancellation in the context of Combine:

Error Handling:

1. **Handling Errors in Operators:**

· Combine provides operators that can handle errors, such as **mapError**, **catch**, and **replaceError**.
· Use these operators to transform, catch, or replace errors in the pipeline.

```swift
let cancellable =
URLSession.shared.dataTaskPublisher(for: url)
    .tryMap { data, response in
        guard let httpResponse = response as?
        HTTPURLResponse, httpResponse.statusCode ==
        200 else {
            throw URLError(.badServerResponse)
        }
        return data
    }
    .sink(
        receiveCompletion: { completion in
            switch completion {
            case .finished:
                print("Request completed
                successfully.")
            case .failure(let error):
                print("Error: \(error)")
            }
        },
        receiveValue: { data in
            // Handle successful data
        }
    )
```

1. **Handling Errors in Subscribers:**

- Use the **receive** method in subscribers to handle errors when receiving values.
- The **receive(completion:)** method is called when the publisher completes with either success or failure.

```
let cancellable = somePublisher
    .sink(
        receiveCompletion: { completion in
            switch completion {
            case .finished:
                print("Request completed
                successfully.")
            case .failure(let error):
                print("Error: \(error)")
            }
        },
        receiveValue: { value in
            // Handle successful value
        }
    )
```

1. **Error Types:**

- Combine uses the **Error** protocol for representing errors.
- You can use built-in error types or create custom error types that conform to the **Error** protocol.

```
enum NetworkingError: Error {
    case invalidURL
    case serverError
}
```

Cancellation:

1. Cancellable:

- The **sink** operator returns a **Cancellable** object, which represents the subscription.
- You can store the cancellable and use it to cancel the subscription.

```
let cancellable = somePublisher
    .sink { value in
        // Handle value
    }
```

1. Cancelling Subscriptions:

- Use the **cancel** method on the **Cancellable** object to cancel the subscription.

```
cancellable.cancel()
```

1. **Lifetime of Subscriptions:**

· Subscriptions live as long as there is a strong reference to them.
· If the subscriber or publisher is deinitialized, the subscription is automatically cancelled.

```
var cancellables: Set<AnyCancellable> = []

somePublisher
    .sink { value in
        // Handle value
    }
    .store(in: &cancellables)
```

1. **Using store(in:):**

· The **store(in:)** method is a convenient way to store cancellables in a collection.
· This helps manage the lifetime of subscriptions and automatically cancels them when the collection is deallocated.

```
somePublisher
    .sink { value in
        // Handle value
    }
    .store(in: &cancellables)
```

Understanding error handling and cancellation in Combine is

crucial for writing robust and reliable asynchronous code. It allows you to gracefully handle errors and manage the lifecycle of subscriptions, preventing memory leaks and ensuring the efficient use of resources.

13

Combine Advanced Topics

Combine Advanced Topics: Explore advanced Combine concepts like custom publishers and operators.

Combine is a powerful framework in Swift for handling asynchronous and event-driven code. In addition to the basic concepts of publishers, subscribers, and operators, there are advanced topics in Combine that involve creating custom publishers and operators. Here's an exploration of these advanced Combine concepts:

1. Custom Publishers:

- Combine provides a set of built-in publishers, but you can create custom publishers to model specific behaviors.
- To create a custom publisher, you need to conform to the **Publisher** protocol and implement the **subscribe** method.

Example of a Custom Publisher:

```
import Combine

struct CustomPublisher: Publisher {
    typealias Output = String
    typealias Failure = Never

    func receive<S>(subscriber: S) where S :
    Subscriber, Failure == S.Failure, Output ==
    S.Input {
        let subscription =
        CustomSubscription(subscriber: subscriber)
        subscriber.receive(subscription: subscription)
    }
}

struct CustomSubscription<S: Subscriber>:
Subscription where S.Input == String {
    private var subscriber: S

    init(subscriber: S) {
        self.subscriber = subscriber
    }

    func request(_ demand: Subscribers.Demand) {
        // Generate and send values based on demand
        for _ in 0..<demand {
            _ = subscriber.receive("Data")
        }

        // Indicate completion when necessary
        subscriber.receive(completion: .finished)
    }

    func cancel() {
```

```
        // Perform cleanup when subscription is
        cancelled
    }
}
```

2. Custom Operators:

- Combine allows you to create custom operators to transform or combine values in a pipeline.
- Conforming to the **Operator** protocol involves defining the **Body** type, which represents the transformation applied to the upstream publisher.

Example of a Custom Operator:

```
import Combine

struct CustomOperator: Operator {
    typealias Input = String
    typealias Output = String

    func receive<Downstream: Subscriber>(subscriber:
    Downstream) where Downstream.Failure == Never,
    Downstream.Input == String {
        let subscription =
        CustomOperatorSubscription(downstream:
        subscriber)
        subscriber.receive(subscription: subscription)
    }
}
```

```
struct CustomOperatorSubscription<Downstream:
Subscriber>: Subscription where Downstream.Input ==
String, Downstream.Failure == Never {
    private var downstream: Downstream

    init(downstream: Downstream) {
        self.downstream = downstream
    }

    func request(_ demand: Subscribers.Demand) {
        // Apply the custom transformation and send
        values downstream
        for _ in 0..<demand {
            _ = downstream.receive("Transformed Data")
        }

        // Indicate completion when necessary
        downstream.receive(completion: .finished)
    }

    func cancel() {
        // Perform cleanup when subscription is
        cancelled
    }
}
```

3. Understanding Backpressure:

- Backpressure is the mechanism through which subscribers communicate their readiness to receive more values.
- Combine handles backpressure automatically, but when creating custom publishers, it's important to consider how to respond to demand.

Example of Backpressure Handling:

```
func request(_ demand: Subscribers.Demand) {
    // Only send values based on the received demand
    for _ in 0..<demand {
        if shouldSendValue {
            _ = downstream.receive("Data")
        }
    }
}
```

4. Error Handling in Custom Publishers:

- Custom publishers can also handle errors by sending a completion event with a failure.
- Use **subscriber.receive(completion:)** to send a completion event.

Example of Error Handling:

```
func request(_ demand: Subscribers.Demand) {
    do {
        // Perform operations and handle errors
        try performOperation()

        // Send values based on demand
        for _ in 0..<demand {
            _ = downstream.receive("Data")
        }
```

```
        // Indicate completion when necessary
        downstream.receive(completion: .finished)
    } catch {
        // Send an error event to the downstream
        subscriber
        downstream.receive(completion:
        .failure(error))
    }
}
```

These advanced Combine concepts allow you to create custom publishers and operators tailored to your specific use cases. When working with Combine, understanding these advanced topics can enhance your ability to model complex asynchronous workflows and data transformations.

14

Integration with UIKit and App Architecture

Integration with UIKit and App Architecture: Learn how to integrate SwiftUI with existing UIKit code.

Integrating SwiftUI with existing UIKit code is a common scenario, especially when adopting SwiftUI in an app that already uses UIKit. SwiftUI provides a way to seamlessly integrate with UIKit through the **UIHostingController** and **UIViewControllerR epresentable** protocols. Here's how you can integrate SwiftUI with UIKit:

1. UIHostingController:

- Use **UIHostingController** to wrap a SwiftUI view and present it in a UIKit-based view controller.
- This allows you to embed SwiftUI views into your existing UIKit-based navigation controllers, tab controllers, or other

view controllers.

```
import SwiftUI

struct MySwiftUIView: View {
    var body: some View {
        Text("Hello, SwiftUI!")
    }
}

// Create a UIHostingController to wrap the SwiftUI
view
let hostingController = UIHostingController(rootView:
MySwiftUIView())
```

2. UIViewControllerRepresentable:

- Conform to the **UIViewControllerRepresentable** protocol
  to create a SwiftUI representation of a UIKit view controller.
- This allows you to use UIKit-based view controllers within
  SwiftUI hierarchies.

```
import SwiftUI

struct MyUIKitViewController:
UIViewControllerRepresentable {
    func makeUIViewController(context: Context) ->
    UIViewController {
        return MyUIKitViewController()
    }
```

```
func updateUIViewController(_ uiViewController:
UIViewController, context: Context) {
    // Update the UIKit view controller if needed
}
}
```

3. Passing Data between SwiftUI and UIKit:

- Use **@Binding** or **@State** to pass data between SwiftUI views and UIKit view controllers.
- You can also use **ObservableObject** and **@Published** to create a shared data model.

```
class SharedData: ObservableObject {
    @Published var message: String = "Hello from
    SwiftUI!"
}

struct MySwiftUIView: View {
    @ObservedObject var sharedData: SharedData

    var body: some View {
        Text(sharedData.message)
    }
}

// Use the shared data in UIKit view controller
let sharedData = SharedData()
let hostingController = UIHostingController(rootView:
MySwiftUIView(sharedData: sharedData))
```

4. *Handling UIKit Delegates:*

· If your SwiftUI view relies on UIKit delegates, conform to the delegate protocols in your **UIViewControllerRepresentable** implementation.

```
import SwiftUI

struct MyUIKitViewController:
UIViewControllerRepresentable {
    func makeUIViewController(context: Context) ->
    UIViewController {
        let viewController = MyUIKitViewController()
        viewController.delegate = context.coordinator
        return viewController
    }

    func updateUIViewController(_ uiViewController:
    UIViewController, context: Context) {
        // Update the UIKit view controller if needed
    }

    func makeCoordinator() -> Coordinator {
        Coordinator(self)
    }

    class Coordinator: NSObject {
        var parent: MyUIKitViewController

        init(_ parent: MyUIKitViewController) {
            self.parent = parent
        }

        // Implement UIKit delegate methods
    }
```

88

```
}
```

5. SwiftUI within UIKit Navigation:

- Embed SwiftUI views within UIKit navigation controllers using **UIHostingController**.

```
let hostingController = UIHostingController(rootView:
MySwiftUIView())
navigationController.pushViewController(hostingController,
animated: true)
```

6. UIKit within SwiftUI Navigation:

- Integrate UIKit-based view controllers within SwiftUI navigation hierarchies using **UIViewControllerRepresentable**.

```
NavigationView {
    VStack {
        Text("SwiftUI View")
        MyUIKitViewController()
    }
}
```

By leveraging **UIHostingController** and **UIViewControllerRepr esentable**, you can seamlessly integrate SwiftUI with existing UIKit code. This flexibility allows you to adopt SwiftUI gradually in UIKit-based projects or use UIKit components within SwiftUI-based projects.

Understand how SwiftUI fits into different app architectures.

SwiftUI is a modern, declarative framework for building user interfaces across all Apple platforms. It can be integrated into different app architectures, including MVC (Model-View-Controller), MVVM (Model-View-ViewModel), and even architectures that incorporate SwiftUI's principles with Combine. Let's explore how SwiftUI fits into these app architectures:

1. Model-View-Controller (MVC):

- **Model:** Represents the data and business logic of the app.
- **View:** Displays the user interface and communicates user interactions to the controller.
- **Controller:** Manages the flow of data between the model and the view, handling user inputs and updating the model.

How SwiftUI Fits In:

- SwiftUI can be used to define the views and part of the controllers.
- Views are described declaratively, and changes in the model automatically update the view.

90

2. Model-View-ViewModel (MVVM):

- **Model:** Represents the data and business logic.
- **View:** Displays the user interface.
- **ViewModel:** Acts as an intermediary between the model and the view, preparing the data for presentation and handling user interactions.

How SwiftUI Fits In:

- SwiftUI can be used for the view layer.
- Combine framework is often used with SwiftUI to facilitate reactive data binding between the ViewModel and the View.

3. Combine + SwiftUI Architecture:

- Combine is a framework for processing values over time. It's often used in conjunction with SwiftUI.
- Publishers emit values, and subscribers receive and react to these values.

How SwiftUI Fits In:

- Combine integrates seamlessly with SwiftUI, enabling reactive programming patterns.
- SwiftUI's declarative syntax aligns well with Combine's principles.

4. Redux Architecture:

- Redux is a state management pattern commonly used with web frameworks like React.
- The state of the app is kept in a single, immutable data store. Actions trigger state changes through reducers.

How SwiftUI Fits In:

- SwiftUI can be used for the view layer.
- Combine can be used for handling state changes and managing app-wide data flow.

5. Clean Architecture:

- Clean Architecture promotes separation of concerns by dividing the app into layers: presentation, domain, and data.
- The inner layers are independent of the outer layers.

How SwiftUI Fits In:

- SwiftUI is often used for the presentation layer.
- Combine can be used to handle interactions between the presentation and domain layers.

6. VIPER Architecture:

- VIPER stands for View, Interactor, Presenter, Entity, and Routing.
- Each component has a specific responsibility, making the architecture highly modular.

How SwiftUI Fits In:

- SwiftUI can be used for the view layer.
- Combine and other Swift frameworks can be used for the interactions between the components.

7. Coordinators:

- The Coordinator pattern involves using coordinator objects to manage the flow of navigation and presentation.

How SwiftUI Fits In:

- SwiftUI views can be embedded in a **UIHostingController** and coordinated using UIKit coordinators.

8. Hybrid Architectures:

- In many cases, apps use a combination of different architectural patterns to meet specific needs.

How SwiftUI Fits In:

- SwiftUI can be integrated as the view layer in hybrid architectures.

Overall, SwiftUI is versatile and can be integrated into various app architectures. Its declarative syntax, reactive programming capabilities, and seamless integration with Combine make it a powerful choice for building modern and maintainable user interfaces. The specific integration points will depend on the architectural patterns and frameworks chosen for other parts of the app.

15

Real-world Projects

Real-world Projects: Apply your knowledge by building small to medium-sized projects.

Building real-world projects is an excellent way to apply your knowledge and gain practical experience with SwiftUI. Below are some project ideas with varying complexity that you can work on to hone your SwiftUI skills:

1. Task Manager App:

- **Features:**
- Create, read, update, and delete tasks.
- Categorize tasks into different lists.
- Set due dates and priorities for tasks.
- **Learning Focus:**
- Navigation in SwiftUI.
- List and Form views.

- Data persistence using Core Data or UserDefaults.

2. Weather App:

- **Features:**
- Fetch and display weather information for a given location.
- Include current weather, hourly forecast, and daily forecast.
- Use a third-party API to get real-time weather data.
- **Learning Focus:**
- Networking in SwiftUI.
- Parsing JSON data.
- Handling asynchronous tasks.

3. Expense Tracker:

- **Features:**
- Log daily expenses.
- Categorize expenses (food, transportation, etc.).
- View monthly or yearly spending trends.
- **Learning Focus:**
- User interface for data input.
- Data visualization using charts.
- Data modeling and storage.

4. Photo Gallery App:

- **Features:**
- Browse and display photos.
- Allow users to add captions and tags to photos.
- Implement a search feature based on tags.
- **Learning Focus:**

- Working with images in SwiftUI.
- Handling user input gestures.
- Implementing search functionality.

5. *Chat Application:*

- **Features:**
- Real-time messaging between users.
- Display online/offline status.
- Implement user authentication.
- **Learning Focus:**
- WebSocket communication.
- User authentication and authorization.
- Real-time updates using Combine.

6. *Recipe App:*

- **Features:**
- Browse and search for recipes.
- View detailed recipe information, including ingredients and steps.
- Allow users to save favorite recipes.
- **Learning Focus:**
- Complex UI layouts in SwiftUI.
- Data modeling for recipes.
- User interactions and animations.

7. Fitness Tracking App:

- **Features:**
- Log daily workouts.
- Track progress over time.
- Implement a simple calendar for viewing workout history.
- **Learning Focus:**
- Custom UI for workout tracking.
- Calendar implementation.
- Charting and visualizing data.

8. To-Do List with Reminders:

- **Features:**
- Create tasks with due dates.
- Implement local notifications for reminders.
- Allow users to mark tasks as completed.
- **Learning Focus:**
- Local notifications in SwiftUI.
- Handling background tasks.
- Integrating with iOS reminders.

9. Social Media Feed:

- **Features:**
- Display a feed of user posts.
- Allow users to like and comment on posts.
- Implement infinite scrolling for the feed.
- **Learning Focus:**
- Dynamic UI based on data.
- Implementing likes and comments.

- Efficiently loading and displaying large datasets.

10. *Expense Splitting App:*

- **Features:**
- Track shared expenses among a group of friends.
- Automatically calculate who owes money to whom.
- Allow users to settle debts.
- **Learning Focus:**
- Algorithm for splitting expenses.
- Handling complex state and data relationships.
- Implementing a clean and intuitive user interface.

As you work on these projects, you'll encounter various challenges that will help reinforce your understanding of SwiftUI concepts and encourage you to explore different aspects of app development. Additionally, consider incorporating good software development practices, such as code organization, version control, and testing, to enhance the overall quality of your projects.

Experiment with SwiftUI in personal or open-source projects.

Experimenting with SwiftUI in personal or open-source projects is a great way to deepen your understanding of the framework and contribute to the SwiftUI community. Here are some suggestions on how you can experiment with SwiftUI in your projects:

1. Create a Custom SwiftUI Component:

- Build a custom SwiftUI component that can be reused across different projects.
- Examples include a custom navigation bar, a date picker with additional features, or a unique animated button.

2. Integrate SwiftUI with Core Data:

- Explore how SwiftUI interacts with Core Data for data persistence.
- Create a project where you can perform CRUD (Create, Read, Update, Delete) operations on a Core Data model using SwiftUI.

3. Explore SwiftUI Animations:

- Dive into SwiftUI animations and create a project where you experiment with different animation styles and techniques.
- Build an interactive onboarding experience with captivating animations.

4. Develop a SwiftUI-based Dashboard:

- Create a dashboard application using SwiftUI to display data analytics or statistics.
- Experiment with different chart libraries integrated into SwiftUI for visual representation.

5. Build a SwiftUI-based Game:

- Create a simple game using SwiftUI, such as a card-matching game or a puzzle game.
- Implement game logic, animations, and user interactions.

6. Adopt Dark Mode and Accessibility:

- Implement Dark Mode in your existing projects or create a new project that fully supports Dark Mode.
- Explore SwiftUI's accessibility features to make your projects more inclusive.

7. Experiment with SwiftUI Grids:

- Build a project that involves displaying data in a grid format using SwiftUI.
- Explore different grid styles, adaptive layouts, and responsiveness.

8. Implement SwiftUI Navigation Patterns:

- Experiment with SwiftUI navigation patterns, such as tab bars, navigation stacks, and modal presentations.
- Create a project that showcases smooth and intuitive navigation.

9. Integrate SwiftUI with Networking:

- Build a project that fetches data from a RESTful API using SwiftUI.
- Experiment with asynchronous data loading, error handling, and displaying dynamic content.

10. Contribute to SwiftUI Open Source Projects:

- Explore existing SwiftUI open-source projects on platforms like GitHub.
- Contribute bug fixes, enhancements, or new features to gain experience collaborating with others.

11. Create a SwiftUI macOS App:

- Build a macOS application using SwiftUI.
- Experiment with adapting your SwiftUI components to the larger screen and implementing macOS-specific features.

12. Experiment with SwiftUI Combine Integration:

- Combine is a powerful framework for handling asynchronous events. Integrate Combine with SwiftUI in a project to explore reactive programming concepts.

13. Implement a SwiftUI-based Blog or Portfolio:

- Create a personal blog or portfolio website using SwiftUI.
- Showcase your projects, skills, and achievements.

14. Explore SwiftUI for watchOS:

- Build a watchOS app using SwiftUI to understand how the framework adapts to the smaller screen and limited input methods.

15. Participate in SwiftUI Challenges:

- Join SwiftUI challenges on social media platforms or community forums.
- Complete challenges to explore new concepts and receive feedback from the community.

Experimenting with SwiftUI in various types of projects will help you gain practical experience and deepen your understanding of the framework. Whether it's creating custom components, exploring animations, or contributing to open-source projects, the hands-on experience will enhance your SwiftUI skills.

16

Community and Resources:

Community and Resources: Engage with the SwiftUI community through forums, blogs, and social media.

Engaging with the SwiftUI community through forums, blogs, and social media is an excellent way to stay updated on the latest developments, learn new tips and tricks, and connect with other developers. Here are some resources and platforms where you can actively participate in the SwiftUI community:

1. Forums:

- **Swift.org Forums:** The official Swift forums hosted by the Swift community. You can find dedicated sections for SwiftUI discussions, announcements, and help.
- Swift.org Forums - SwiftUI
- **Stack Overflow:** A popular Q&A platform where developers ask and answer questions. The SwiftUI tag on Stack Overflow

is an active space for problem-solving and knowledge sharing.
- Stack Overflow - SwiftUI

2. Blogs and Tutorials:

- **Swift by Sundell:** John Sundell's blog provides in-depth articles and tutorials on Swift and SwiftUI. It's a great resource for both beginners and experienced developers.
- Swift by Sundell
- **Hacking with Swift:** Paul Hudson's website offers a vast collection of Swift and SwiftUI tutorials. It includes hands-on projects and challenges to enhance your skills.
- Hacking with Swift
- **Donny Wals Blog:** Donny Wals writes insightful blog posts about Swift, SwiftUI, and iOS development. His articles often cover practical tips and real-world scenarios.
- Donny Wals Blog

3. Social Media:

- **Twitter:** Follow SwiftUI experts, developers, and organizations on Twitter to stay updated on the latest news, tips, and discussions. Use hashtags like #SwiftUI to discover relevant content.
- Example accounts: @SwiftLang, @twostraws, @johnsundell
- **LinkedIn:** Join SwiftUI and iOS development groups on LinkedIn to connect with professionals in the field. Participate in discussions and share your own experiences.

4. GitHub:

- **GitHub Repositories:** Explore open-source SwiftUI projects on GitHub to learn from others' code and contribute to collaborative efforts. You can find interesting projects, libraries, and utilities.
- Example repositories: Awesome SwiftUI, SwiftUI-Cheat-Sheet
- **SwiftUI Gists:** Check out SwiftUI-related gists on GitHub for quick code snippets and solutions to common problems.
- GitHub Gist - SwiftUI

5. YouTube and Podcasts:

- **YouTube Channels:** Subscribe to YouTube channels dedicated to SwiftUI and iOS development. Video tutorials and walkthroughs can provide visual explanations.
- Example channels: CodeWithChris, Sean Allen
- **iOS Development Podcasts:** Listen to podcasts that cover SwiftUI and iOS development. Podcasts are a great way to stay informed while commuting or doing other tasks.
- Example podcasts: Swift by Sundell, iPhreaks

Engaging with the SwiftUI community is not only a way to learn but also an opportunity to share your experiences and contribute to the collective knowledge. By actively participating in discussions, asking questions, and sharing insights, you can build connections and stay at the forefront of SwiftUI development trends.

Stay updated with SwiftUI

Staying updated with SwiftUI involves keeping track of the latest releases, updates, and best practices. Here are some strategies to stay current with SwiftUI developments:

1. Official Documentation and Release Notes:

- Regularly check the official SwiftUI documentation on Apple's developer website for up-to-date information.
- Explore release notes for SwiftUI and related frameworks to understand new features, improvements, and bug fixes.

2. Swift Blog and Announcements:

- Follow the official Swift blog for announcements related to the Swift programming language, including SwiftUI updates.
- Subscribe to newsletters or feeds that curate Swift and SwiftUI-related news.

3. Social Media and Forums:

- Follow relevant accounts on Twitter, including official Swift and SwiftUI accounts, influential developers, and iOS development communities.
- Participate in SwiftUI discussions on platforms like the Swift.org Forums and Stack Overflow.

4. Online Communities and Meetups:

- Join online communities such as the Swift.org forums, Swift Language Community on Discord, or iOS development groups on platforms like LinkedIn.
- Attend virtual or local meetups focused on Swift and SwiftUI.

5. Blogs and Tutorials:

- Regularly read blogs and tutorials from prominent SwiftUI developers and educators.
- Subscribe to websites like Swift by Sundell, Hacking with Swift, and others for in-depth articles and tutorials.

6. GitHub Repositories:

- Explore and star SwiftUI-related repositories on GitHub to receive notifications about updates.
- Contribute to open-source SwiftUI projects to stay engaged with the community.

7. Podcasts and YouTube Channels:

- Listen to iOS development podcasts and watch YouTube channels that frequently cover SwiftUI topics.
- Subscribe to channels like CodeWithChris, Sean Allen, and others for video content.

8. Apple Developer Conferences:

- Attend Apple's annual developer conferences, such as WWDC (Worldwide Developers Conference), where Apple announces major updates to SwiftUI.
- Watch session videos related to SwiftUI from past conferences on the Apple Developer website.

9. Books and Courses:

- Read books and take online courses focused on SwiftUI to gain comprehensive knowledge.
- Explore resources like the Ray Wenderlich SwiftUI Tutorials for structured learning.

10. Experiment and Build Projects:

- Actively experiment with SwiftUI by building small projects, trying out new features, and implementing best practices.
- Stay hands-on to discover nuances and understand practical usage.

By combining these strategies, you can create a well-rounded approach to stay updated with SwiftUI. Consistently exploring official documentation, engaging with the community, and experimenting with real-world projects will ensure you remain at the forefront of SwiftUI development.